WHSmith

Revise
English

KS3: YEAR 9
Book 2

Age 13–14

Roger Machin

First published in 2007
exclusively for WHSmith by
Hodder Murray, a member of the Hodder Headline group
338 Euston Road
London
NW1 3BH

Impression number   10 9 8 7 6 5 4 3 2 1
Year   2011 2010 2009 2008 2007
Text © Hodder Education 2007

All text extracts written by the author, unless otherwise acknowledged.

A CIP record for this book is available from the British Library.

Cover illustration by Sally Newton Illustrations

Typeset by GreenGate Publishing Services, Tonbridge, Kent

ISBN-13: 978 0 340 94304 5

Printed and bound in Italy.

Contents

How to use this book

The fact that you are choosing to read these words means you are thinking about improving your English. Congratulations! This is the first step towards success and you have taken it already. Your desire to succeed is the essential ingredient to progress. Think of this book as your partner, your personal trainer, in your quest to achieve.

Key Stage 3

Key Stage 3 (you'll often see it called just KS3) is the name given to Years 7, 8 and 9. Students in KS3 are normally aged between 11 and 14 years old. It is a crucial time for all subjects and no less so for English. It is the time when the lessons learned from junior school are built upon and when the foundations are laid for study up to GCSE. Almost all students do the compulsory KS3 test at the end of Year 9. Many schools now opt to take similar tests at the end of Years 7 and 8.

English at KS3

The English tests at KS3 assess students in two basic areas: their ability to read and write. Teachers assess the other two components of English (speaking and listening) separately. Students are expected to read lots of different sorts of texts (for example, stories, newspapers, biographies) and to show their understanding of them. They are expected to demonstrate that they can write in a variety of ways (for example, imaginatively, persuasively, informatively) and in good English. This book, along with the other five books in this series, covers every single one of the skills you need to achieve the best you possibly can in the English tests.

Revision

Many students think of revision as something they do just before a test takes place. Don't be one of them! Success is based on continual revision, just a little every day. Go over what you know. Check, recheck and identify areas of difficulty. Practise what you're good at and get help in areas where you're weaker. Let this book be your friend and companion in this process. An exercise every day or two – more if you're enjoying yourself – will be enough to build up your confidence and ability. Successful revision is like effective physical training: it needs to be gradual.

The *Revise KS3 English* family

This book is one of a family of six books designed to improve your performance in English at KS3. There are two books for each year group and 26 units in each book. Each unit focuses on one of the skills you will need to learn or revise as you progress from Year 7 through to Year 9. Once you feel confident in the skills revised in the Year 7 books you can move on up to Year 8. It doesn't matter which year group you are actually in. Neither does it matter if you are in Year 9 and you want to use the Year 7 books as kick-starters. Use the books that you feel comfortable with and go with your instincts.

Using this book

Work through the units in the order they appear. In other words, start with Unit 1 and finish with Unit 26. The reason for this is that the skills learned and revised earlier in the book are built upon as the text progresses. There is no fixed time limit for each unit although you should be able to finish most of them in a single sitting. Towards the end of each of the units you will find a more challenging section (shaded in mauve). This section is designed to help you push yourself that little bit further in the direction of understanding and success. The Revision booster boxes and Revision tips at the side also help with your study.

Home study tips

You'll discover fairly quickly that the answers are at the end of the book! Try not to look at them until you have worked as hard as you possibly can on the unit. The fact that you are working at home means you are eager to improve and to get ahead. You're not going to do this if you take the easy way out. Engage with what you read, and write answers as fully and in as much detail as you can. Remember that you are taking responsibility for your own learning. Not many students do this and if you do it properly it is going to give you an advantage.

If you work steadily through this book and the other books in the series your English will improve. This is a definite, cast-iron and unarguable fact. It might seem hard at first, especially if you're tired after a long day's work. But stick with it. Mental stamina, just like physical stamina, improves with exercise. Don't get downhearted if you can't complete an exercise. Give it your best shot and if you're still stuck in a rut, move on to another unit. Remember that the best way to get ahead is to get started and you're about to get started right now!

1: Phrases in sentences

In this unit you will learn
▶ to arrange structures within sentences

Get started

Words relating to a noun (including the noun itself) are known together as a **noun phrase**. The following show how noun phrases can be built, related to *water*.

● *water*

● *the water*

● *the sparkling water*

● *some pure, sparkling water*

Water counts as a noun phrase even though it is only one word.

Practice

1. Make three noun phrases of your own related to the word *sugar*.

   In this sentence there are two noun phrases.

   The angry horse leapt the broken fence.

   The first noun phrase is *the angry horse*.

   The second noun phrase is *the broken fence*.

2. Write out the noun phrases in the following sentences.

   The eagle grabbed the unlucky rabbit.

   Mr Aggarwal flew the airship.

   Bright stones littered the beach.

   The structure, noun phrase + verb + noun phrase is common. The following are some more examples of this pattern.

   The baby eats mud.

   Many insects build complicated homes.

   Large planes cause serious pollution.

3. In the three sentences above, identify

   a the six noun phrases

   b the three verbs

Connectives can be used to extend this basic sentence structure. Connectives are words that bolt together different parts of a sentence. They include words like

and   because   so   while   before   after   when   though   if   until

These connectives enable writers to join two parts of a sentence like this.

The baby eats mud while her mother cuts the grass.

The structure of this sentence is
NP + verb + NP + connective + NP + verb + NP

4 Write down the structures of each of the following sentences.

a *The farmer works the fields while his children play.*

b *Amit dances if his brother sings.*

c *Jana did the shopping until Freddy left school.*

On either side of a connective there are two clauses. A **clause** is a part of a sentence that contains a verb. In the first sentence above, *The farmer works the fields* is the first clause and *his children play* is the second clause.

5 Write out the four clauses in the other two sentences in question 4.

Sentences can be given more variety by altering the position of the clauses they contain. The first (**main**) and second (**subordinate**) clauses in the sentences above can swap position to make the following.

While his children play, the farmer works the fields.

If his brother sings, Amit dances.

Until Freddy left school, Jana did the shopping.

Notice that the connective goes to the start of the sentence along with the subordinate clause. Also notice that a comma is used to separate the clauses when the connective has been moved.

6 Alter the positions of the main and subordinate clauses in the following sentences.

a The city fell as the army entered.

b The eagle swooped before the rabbit could escape.

c Dig a hole if there's no other way through.

d I can't leave until she arrives.

How did I do?

I know how to arrange structures within sentences.

Connectives add variety and length to sentences.

2: Noun phrases

In this unit you will learn
- to develop noun phrases

Get started

Remember that a noun phrase can be made up of one or more words. It can be a pronoun, a single noun, or a group of words related to a noun. Look at the following examples.

- *it*   a single pronoun

- *salt*   a single noun

- *some paper*   a determiner + a noun

- *the grey wolf*   a determiner + an adjective + a noun

Taken together, any one of these four words/word combinations is called a noun phrase.

As a writer, it is important that you vary your use of noun phrases. Sometimes it is a good thing to use pronouns or single-word nouns as your noun phrase. At other times, well-developed noun phrases are excellent for providing lots of detail in a compressed way.

Practice

1   Add an appropriate noun to each of the determiners and adjectives below.

Many   A rusty   These new   That broken   The cold

2   a   What are the five determiners in the list above?

     b   What are the four adjectives?

Notice that, on their own, determiners and adjectives provide the reader with no sensible information. A noun is needed to give these words something to refer to.

Noun phrases can be extended and linked by using **prepositions**. Here is a list of words often used as prepositions.

in   on   under   beyond   with   at   through   up   of   over

They work within noun phrases in the following way.

The grey wolf with the bloody teeth

3   Identify each of the prepositions linking the noun phrases below.

     a   The dark behind the curtains

     b   Some dust on that high ledge

c That politician with the good ideas

d A day at the races

e The fury of the crashing waves

All noun phrases (including the linked phrases above) can be used as the subjects of sentences. The **subject** of a sentence is the thing or person doing the action of the verb. You can find the subject of the sentence by asking who or what *does* the verb. Look at the examples below.

The grey wolf howled.

It trickled.

A politician spoke.

To find the subjects of the verbs you need to ask

Who/What howled?	*The grey wolf*	is the subject of the verb.
Who/What trickled?	*It*	is the subject of the verb.
Who/What spoke?	*A politician*	is the subject of the verb.

Find the (noun phrase) subjects of the verbs in the following sentences. Use the examples above to guide you. Remember that the noun phrase can be a single word or a group of words.

a He arrived.

b That old suit of armour moved.

c Good ideas survive.

d The man with the loud voice shouted.

e The shadows drifted.

Revision booster

Look at the following list of noun phrases. Add a single-word verb to each of them so that they become subjects of the sentences you create.

a The screeching baby

b A man with a black beard

c The mobile phone

How did I do?

I can develop noun phrases.　　　　 ☐

3: Structuring information

In this unit you will learn
▷ to assess informative prose

Get started

Read the following extract from a passage about Tyrannosaurus.

The name Tyrannosaurus, from ancient Greek, means tyrant lizard. Most people nowadays refer to this great dinosaur more simply as T Rex. This extraordinary beast has captured our imagination perhaps more than any other animal that has walked the Earth. It was a true giant. Its head was the size of a fully grown human. It stood as high as a double decker bus. But it is its reputation as a fearful predator which has held us in awe since its discovery over one hundred years ago.

Remember that a noun phrase is a group of words used together to refer to a noun. Noun phrases can be on their own, or they can be linked with prepositions. Look at the following examples.

they   a pronoun

some people   a determiner combined with a noun

many people in the museum   two noun phrases joined with a preposition

Sometimes noun phrases are used in **apposition**. This means they are placed adjacent, usuallly sectioned off with commas. Look at the following sentences. They both contain noun phrases in apposition.

Our black dog, Hercules, came running up the path.

Caesar, the name of the Roman emperor, is the root of Kaiser and Tsar.

In these examples, the second noun phrase is used to give extra detail about the first noun phrase.

(!) **Use appositional noun phrases in your own writing to provide detail and variety.**

Practice

1 Write down the two noun phrases used in apposition in the sentences above.

Notice that the second noun phrase in the pair needs to be sectioned off with commas.

2 Write down the noun phrase used in apposition in the Tyrannosaurus passage.

When writers make reference to the same thing throughout a text it is often quite hard to avoid repetition of noun phrases. The original noun phrase can be replaced with a pronoun (like *she* or *he* or *it*) but the repetition of pronouns is also to be avoided.

The answer to this problem lies in the imaginative variation of noun phrases. *Different* noun phrases can be used to *refer* to more or less the same thing. A text that uses *varied noun reference* will hold together well and be interesting.

To make all this clearer, look again at the passage about Tyrannosaurus. The simplest way the writer could refer to this dinosaur is either by using the noun *Tyrannosaurus* or the pronoun *it.* A more interesting text, however, has been produced by using varied noun phrases. Here are two of them.

tyrant lizard   this great dinosaur

These two noun phrases refer to the same thing. Repetition has been avoided by using different noun phrases to do it.

As with all informative writing, the Tyrannosaurus passage provides facts.

3 What facts do we discover about the following two details?

a the language the word *Tyrannosaurus* comes from

b when Tyrannosaurus was first discovered

Facts about unfamiliar things can often be made clearer with the use of comparisons. For example, few people would be able to picture a Diplodocus' brain if it were expressed in metric terms. Everyone, however, can imagine the brain if it is described as a comparison.

A Diplodocus' brain was no larger than a human's clenched fist.

The Tyrannosaurus passage makes comparisons like this twice.

4 What are the head size and height of Tyrannosaurus compared to?

Revision booster

5 Find as many noun phrases as you can in the extract that refer to Tyrannosaurus. Include the two noun phrases provided above. Only include noun phrases that refer to the animal itself. Do not include references to parts of its body.

How did I do?

I know how to assess informative prose.   ✔ ☐

4: Verb forms

Get started

So far in this book you have looked mainly at noun phrases. You know that noun phrases can be built up in the following ways.

- *it*   a pronoun
- *fire*   a noun
- *that tight string*   a noun with additions like determiners and adjectives
- *the cold tap in the kitchen*   a pair of noun phrases joined by a preposition

You know that any of these noun phrase variants can be used as the subject of a verb.

it rains

fire glows

that tight string snapped

the cold tap in the kitchen leaks

Remember that the subject of the verb can be identified by asking *who* or *what* did the action of the verb. This works as follows.

Who/What snapped?   *that tight string*   is the subject of the verb.

The most basic form a sentence can usually take is a subject and a verb.

He (the subject) needs a verb (for example, *groans*) to make sense.

Practice

1. In the following three sentences, identify

   a the (noun phrase) subject

   b the verb

   My youngest daughter swims.

   That valuable gold necklace disappeared.

   We arrived.

Like noun phrases, verbs can be made up of either a single word or a group of words. Verbs generally change their form to express different times. Look at the following examples of this.

she swims   (present)

she swam   (past)

she is swimming   (present continuous)

he has swum   (present perfect)

> ! Just like noun phrases, verbs can be made up of one word or more.

2 Using the pronoun *she* as the subject, write each of the following three verbs in the four forms shown above.

a   throw

b   play

c   sing

Notice that each of the verb forms you have used expresses a different point in time. There is normally a close relationship between the verb tense and the real time. Look at these examples.

the dog barked   (past tense to describe past action)

he has arrived   (present perfect to describe a recently competed action)

he is talking   (present continuous to describe an ongoing action)

However, sometimes verb tenses are used very oddly indeed. For example, both the present and the present continuous tenses can be used to describe future actions.

she leaves tomorrow

she is leaving next summer

This can make learning English for foreign language speakers very tricky.

3 In each of the following sentences, identify

a   the (noun phrase) subject

b   the verb

It hurts.

The old black sheep is limping.

Most younger people have stopped.

That broken cistern in the toilet has emptied.

He is teething.

The man in the dark glasses waited.

How did I do?

I know how to work with different verb forms.   ☐

5: Using adverbs

In this unit you will learn
▶ to use adverbs and adverbial phrases

Get started

The main job of **adverbs** is to modify (describe and alter) verbs. Look at the examples below.

The mouse crept silently.

Most of them work hard.

Suddenly, *the bag broke.*

They are eating now.

The ship sank here.

All these adverbs could be removed and the sentences would still make perfect sense.

The mouse crept.

Try removing the adverb from each of the other sentences.

Remember that the basic unit of meaning in almost all sentences is provided by the subject and the verb. The adverb provides an extra layer of detail, not the core.

Notice that the adverbs above have been used to do different sorts of jobs. The first three adverbs describe *how* the action of the verb was performed. The fourth adverb describes *when* the action of the verb takes place. The last adverb describes *where* the action occurs.

Practice

1 Look again at the verbs that have been modified in the sentences above. Write down the verb that has been modified each time. All the verbs, except for the one in the fourth sentence, are a single word long.

Verbs can also be modified with short phrases. These phrases are known as **adverbials** (or **adverbial phrases**) because they do exactly the same job as a single-word adverb. Look at these examples.

She left in a terrible temper.

He arrives at lunchtime.

They walked to the shops.

You can see that these adverbial phrases are very similar to adverbs as they can often be replaced by them.

She left furiously.

He arrives later.

They walked there.

2 Identify and write out the adverbial phrase in each of the following sentences.

a He thought with great speed.

b They drove to their house.

c She is performing in ten minutes.

3 Now replace all the adverbial phrases in question 2 with single adverbs. Choose adverbs that will modify the verb in each sentence in a similar or identical way to the adverbial phrase.

Adverbs and adverbial phrases can often move around within sentences. This means they are useful in creating a variety of sentence structures. Examiners look out for writing that uses a range of structures. It is well worth becoming familiar with the way sections within sentences can be used in different places.

The following sentence demonstrates an adverb being used in a common sort of way.

The door opened slowly.

The adverb *slowly* modifies the verb *opened* to tell the reader something about the way the action (of opening) was performed. The weight of meaning is carried by the subject (*the door*) and the verb (*opened*). This allows the adverb to move freely around in the rest of the sentence.

The door slowly opened.

Slowly, the door opened.

This movable feature of many adverbs gives writers a useful set of options when putting together a variety of sentences.

4 Move the adverb in the following sentence to practise this technique. You should be able to create two new sentence structures from the original. Remember that adverbs at the start of a sentence must be sectioned off with a comma.

The pool emptied quickly.

How did I do?

I can use adverbs and adverbial phrases.

6: Locating detail

In this unit you will learn
  ▶ to locate detail in texts

Get started

This passage is taken from the programme notes for a carnival and procession. The event took place not long ago in Northumberland.

> The carnival officially begins at noon in the town square beside the library. The procession will leave the town centre and will progress gradually towards the sports centre in the park behind Smith Street. By mid-afternoon, the procession will reach the park.

The ability to locate factual information in texts like this is an extremely important skill. You must read closely and extract the precise detail you need.

Practice

1 a What time does the carnival begin?

  b Where exactly is the park?

  c When will the procession reach the park?

Remember that the main job of the adverb is to modify a verb as in the following example.

The train moved slowly.

The adverb *slowly* provides information about the verb *moved.*

2 a Write down the adverb that modifies the verb *begins* in the procession text.

  b Which adverb is used in the second sentence of the text?

  c Which verb does it modify?

Adverbs can provide lots of variety in sentence structure. This is because they can frequently occupy different places within the sentence.

The train slowly moved.

Slowly, the train moved.

3 Look again at the first four words of the procession text. Alter the order of these four words by changing the position of the adverb. Use the two example sentences above to help you.

Recall that adverbial phrases are short phrases that do a similar job to adverbs. Look at the following example of this.

The performances ended simultaneously.

The performances ended at the same time.

The adverb and the adverbial phrase both give information about *when* the action of the verb took place.

In the procession passage, there are two adverbial phrases that provide information about when an action occurs. One of these is

by mid-afternoon

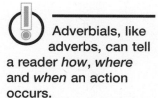

Adverbials, like adverbs, can tell a reader *how, where* and *when* an action occurs.

4 Which other (two-word) adverbial phrase tells the reader *when* an action occurs?

In the first sentence of the passage, there are two adverbial phrases that provide information about *where* the action of the verb *begins* takes place.

5 Write down the two adverbial phrases that tell the reader where this action occurs.

Adverbial phrases can often move around within sentences, just like adverbs, to create a range of effects.

6 Look again at the adverbial phrase in the final sentence of the procession passage. Rewrite the sentence by moving the adverbial phrase to the end.

Recall that verbs can be more than one word in length. This is normally the case with verbs that express future time. The most common method of expressing the future in English is to add the verb *will* before the infinitive of the main verb.

It rained yesterday. It's raining today. It will rain *tomorrow.*

7 Find three examples in the passage of future time being expressed in this way.

Revision booster

Future time, oddly enough, can sometimes be expressed with a present tense verb.

He starts *next week.*

8 Find a single example in the text of future time being expressed in this way.

How did I do?

I know how to locate detail in texts.

7: Parts of verbs

> In this unit you will learn
> ▶ to explore infinitives and participles

Get started

Remember that the basic form of the verb is called the **infinitive**. The infinitive form is the *name* given to each verb. It is used after the modal verbs and the preposition *to*.

be	*must be*	*to be*
mix	*could mix*	*to mix*
go	*shall go*	*to go*

Practice

1 Write out each of the following verbs as a single-word infinitive.

a are laughing

b smiled

c have tried

d is writing

e had eaten

The form taken by a verb can change. This change could be an alteration of spelling. It could also consist of a verb making combinations with other verbs. These changes of form are most often made to express changes in time. Look at the following examples.

I like	(present time)
I liked	(past time)
I will like	(future time)

Check that the following statements are true for the verb *like.*

● The verb looks the same in the infinitive as it does in the present.

● The verb changes to form the past tense.

● The infinitive form is combined with *will* to express the future.

2 The following lists show changes in the forms of the verbs *be* and *go.* Read them and then answer the questions that follow with either *yes* or *no.*

I am	*I go*	(present time)
I was	*I went*	(past time)
I will be	*I will go*	(future time)

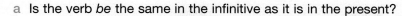

a Is the verb *be* the same in the infinitive as it is in the present?

b Is the verb *go* the same in the infinitive as it is in the present?

c Do the verbs *be* and *go* change to express the past?

d Is the future tense of these verbs formed by adding *will* to the infinitive form?

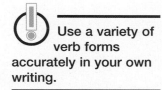

Use a variety of verb forms accurately in your own writing.

Verbs also change their form to become **participles**. There are two participles in English.

The first of these is called the **present/continuous/progressive participle**. It is formed by adding *ing* to the infinitive form of the verb.

be becomes *being*   *have* becomes *having*   *mix* becomes *mixing*

It is used as a continuous verb by combining it with a form of the verb *be*.

I am being *extremely patient.*

We are having *a great time on holiday.*

They were mixing *cement last time I looked.*

Notice that the continuous tenses express actions that *are* or *were* happening.

You can see that a form of the verb *be* makes the first part of continuous tenses. The second part, the continuous participle, is made up of the infinitive plus *ing*.

3 a Write down the three forms of the verb *be* used in the sentences above.

b Write down the infinitive form of each of the three continuous participles.

The second participle used in English is called the **perfect** or **past participle**. It derives from the main verb, often ending with *ed*, and follows a form of the verb *have*.

I have made *a terrible mistake.*

She has arrived *at last.*

It had broken *before he touched it.*

Notice that the perfect tenses express actions that *have* or *had just* finished.

4 a What are the three forms of the verb *have* used in the sentences above?

b What are the infinitive forms of each of the three perfect participles?

How did I do?

I know how to explore infinitives and participles. ☐

8: Biography

Get started

This extract is taken from one of a series of biographical profiles (real life stories) published by a Sunday paper. The passage forms an introduction to the story of William Brown, one of the last British rubber plantation owners to leave Malaysia. At the time of the article, he had returned to Britain to retire. The passage begins with the journalist arriving at William Brown's flat.

It is raining hard as I arrive at William Brown's small flat. I knock on his door and he welcomes me in out of the flood. He is smiling from ear to ear.

"It rained like this every lunchtime in Malaya," he says. "You could set your watch by it."

William Brown left Malaysia (he still calls it by its colonial name, Malaya) five years ago. He had lived there for almost sixty years. During his time there, he witnessed a world war and the collapse of empire. He saw civil unrest and great social change.

"I was playing cricket once against a team from Ipoh," he says. "The opposition captain told me life had improved in Britain. He said I should go back. I told him I was staying. I have had a very happy life. I have done everything I wanted."

Setting a scene can be as important in biography as in fiction. Writers often use the weather to help them set the mood at the beginning of a text.

Practice

1 a What does the writer focus on to set the scene at the start of her article?

b What noun does she use in her second sentence to dramatise the weather?

The reader's first impression of William Brown is gained by something he is doing.

2 a What is William Brown doing?

b What impression does the reader immediately get of him?

Cohesion between paragraphs is an important feature of all texts. Cohesion refers to the way texts hold together and are developed.

3 a What do the first and second paragraphs have in common?

b How is the subject matter moved on by the second paragraph?

People on the page can be brought to life (or **characterised**) by providing the reader with small details about their personalities.

④ Malaysia changed its name from Malaya nearly fifty years ago. The writer characterises William Brown by telling the reader that he still calls it by its colonial name. What impression does this small detail give of William Brown?

⑤ a What game does the writer refer to in the passage?

   b What impression does this detail give of William Brown?

> Small details can tell readers lots about character. Look for them carefully.

Good biographical writing may include a range of verb tenses. This is one way of avoiding a repetitive string of past tense verbs.

He lived *in Malaya. He* owned *a rubber plantation. He* played *cricket. He* returned *to England.*

The writer of the profile avoids this trap. One of her techniques is to use the present tense to talk about past events. This can create the sense of something happening that is immediate and present to the reader.

⑥ Look at the first paragraph.

   a Which two present continuous verbs (two words in length) does the writer use?

   b Find three simple present tense verbs (each one word long) that are used.

Recall the following details of verb construction.

● The present perfect is formed with *have* or *has* before the perfect participle.

● The past perfect is formed with *had* before the perfect participle.

● The past continuous is formed with *was* or *were* before the continuous participle.

⑦ Look at the third and fourth paragraphs of the passage and find the following. Note that each of the verbs you are looking for is formed from the combination of two words.

   a two verbs used in the present perfect tense

   b two verbs used in the past perfect tense

   c two verbs used in the past continuous tense

Look at the way each of these tenses is used in the text. Notice that they help to express time in a very specific way.

How did I do?

I can consider features of biography.   ☐

9: Infinitives

In this unit you will learn
▶ to manipulate verb infinitives

Get started

Recall that the infinitive form of the verb is its root form. Consider the verb *go*. It can take any of the following forms and more.

to go   goes   went   will go   is going   had gone   has gone

The infinitive form, however, is the form by which it is identified. It is the form that is used after the preposition *to* and after a *modal* verb.

Practice

1   a   Which modal verb is the infinitive of the verb *go* used with in the list above?

   b   What is the effect of combining this particular modal verb with an infinitive form?

Modal verbs combine with main verbs. The main verb follows the modal verb. In the example above, *will* is the modal verb that modifies the main verb *go*. Here is a list of common modal verbs.

must   should   ought   could   might   may   will   can   shall   would

2   Look at the first two modals on this list. Combine each of them with the verb *pay*.

   a   Which of the two modals has the stronger impact on the main verb, *pay*?

   b   Find two other modals in the list that can be used with a similar strong effect.

3   Now try to combine the third modal verb with the infinitive *pay*. Which word needs to be placed between this modal verb and an infinitive?

Modal verbs tend to express things like possibility or necessity. For example, you have identified that *must* is used to express a strong need. Look at the way a modal can be used to suggest that something is possible.

We could *try a different solution.*

Modals indicate uncertainty. Even if someone *must* do something it does not mean that they *will* do it. It is for that reason that modals are used to form questions.

Must *I wait until tomorrow?*

Should *we make a complaint?*

4 a Ask a question that begins in the following way

Could he ...

b What happens to the position of the noun subject in this sort of sentence?

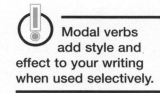

> Modal verbs add style and effect to your writing when used selectively.

Another form of infinitives used on their own at the start of sentences is what are called **imperative clauses**.

Take a break.

Stop doing that.

Come and help us.

Turn on the oven.

Imperatives can be used to provide very clear instructions, directions and requests.

5 Which of the above imperatives might form part of the instructions in a cookery book?

Read the following passage. It shows how imperatives and modal verbs work in a continuous text.

> Clear your desks! Can you come in on Saturday? There's so much to do and it must be out of the way by the end of the weekend. It really would be fantastic to get as many of you as possible. Help us please.

6 Which two imperative clauses are used at the start of sentences in this extract?

Revision booster

Look again at the extract above.

7 a Which modal verb (used here to mean *are you able to?*) starts a question?

b Which modal indicates that it is essential the work is out of the way?

c Which modal describes the situation *if* lots of people come and help?

How did I do?

I know how to manipulate verb infinitives.

10: Creating effects

In this unit you will learn
▶ to write with attitude

Get started

The following text was written by a Year 9 student called Joubin. It describes a man lost at night on a Cornish moor.

> *The mean wind blew chillingly across the moor. A few trees stood stock still in the shadows like naked, broken scarecrows. And then, the light. I stumbled towards it, my eyes blurred. My feet were throbbing, pulsating with pain.*

This is an example of what some examiners call *writing with attitude*. It means putting energy and personality into what is written. This is particularly important with the sort of creative writing displayed in this extract.

An excellent way of giving energy and character to a scene in fiction is by using **personification**. This is a technique that involves treating non-human things as if they were thinking beings.

Practice

1 a Which (three-word) noun phrase in the first sentence of the extract above is used to personify the wind?

b What mood is created in this particular scene by the use of personification?

Remember that adverbs can be used to tell the reader *how* a verb is performed.

2 a What verb is used to relate the action of the wind?

b Which adverb is used to describe this verb?

When texts hold together well they are said to be coherent. An example of coherence is provided by the remark by the narrator that his eyes are *blurred*.

3 How do the narrator's *blurred* eyes tie together with the description in the first sentence?

Alliteration is the technique of using similar sounds close to each other for different effects. This happens in Joubin's second sentence.

4 a Which sounds does the writer use to create alliteration?

b What effect does this create?

The narrator is the imaginary person telling this story. He is the fictional man on the moor, the person referred to in the text as *I*. He is not the same in this particular case as Joubin, the real life author of the story.

Another creative technique used by Joubin is **simile**. Simile is when a comparison is made between two things. In this sort of creative writing, similes are usually meant to create an unusual and striking picture in the reader's mind.

5 What are the trees compared to in Joubin's simile?

Alliteration, simile and personification are all examples of **imagery**. Imagery is the writer's art of creating a picture (an *image*) in the reader's mind. The effect of imagery can be seen by rephrasing some of the central ideas in the extract in a less inventive way.

It was cold.

It was windy.

The man walked over the moor.

He could see a light.

Sometimes these sorts of statements work well. Imagery, however, provides an important variation on this kind of plain English.

In the passage, the writer says it was windy but that the trees were *stock still.*

6

a What does this suggest the trees do not have?

b What adjective later confirms this fact about the trees?

Notice that this is another example of coherence. The text is tied together by elements that relate forwards and backwards to one another.

Revision booster

Reread the following sentence.

And then, the light.

This sentence does not contain a verb. You will generally be taught that sentences must contain a verb, but in your reading you will sometimes come across sentences that don't. If you are going to write sentences like this, you must know what you're doing and keep it to a minimum. It is done quite effectively in the passage above.

7 Rewrite the sentence with a verb of your own choice and contrast the effect.

How did I do?

I know how to write with attitude. ☐

11: Using participles

In this unit you will learn
▶ to vary participle use

Get started

Remember that the *perfect* or *past participle* is a useful form of all English verbs. It combines with either *have, has* or *had* to form the perfect tenses. The regular perfect participle ends with *ed*. But there are many irregular perfect partciples. Look at the following examples.

have go (*have* + infinitive) ——→ *have* gone (*have* + perfect participle)

have try (*have* + infinitive) ——→ *have* tried (*have* + perfect participle)

have be (*have* + infinitive) ——→ *have* been (*have* + perfect participle)

Starting from the infinitive, work out the correct form of the perfect participle.

Practice

1 Look at the following infinitive forms. Write the perfect participle for each.

a think

b stay

c make

d have

e bring

f take

The perfect participle is needed to form the perfect tenses. In terms of time, these are tenses that describe actions recently finished. Look at this example.

I *speak* to her	(simple present)
I *spoke* to her	(simple past)
I *have spoken* to her	(present perfect – the action of speaking is *just* completed)

2 Change the following sentences into the present perfect tense.

a I *buy* stuff online.

b We *eat* snails.

c They *left*.

Many perfect participles can also be used as adjectives. Look at the way the transformation from verb to adjective takes place.

The window has smashed (present perfect sentence – with a verb)

The smashed window (noun phrase – no verb)

Remember that extended noun phrases can be useful because they enable writers to express information in an economical way. Notice that the noun phrase above has provided the writer with the chance to say something else in the sentence.

The smashed window has been mended.

This is in a better style and is more efficient than using two sentences.

The window has smashed. It has been mended.

3 Write out the following perfect tense sentences as noun phrases. Use the perfect participle as an adjective.

 a The earth has dried.

 b These civilisations have fallen.

 c The grapes had ripened.

> **!** Using participles as adjectives is just one way in which writers can express similar ideas in slightly different ways. Be prepared to experiment with these sorts of minor variations. They are key to improving your writing style.

Perfect participles are used to form the perfect tenses. However, they are also used in what are called **passive constructions**. Passive clauses/sentences/constructions are extremely useful. It is well worth learning how and when to use them.

Passives are formed by combining a form of the verb *be* with the past participle of the verb (that you are using to express your idea). Look at the following example.

I broke the window. (active)

The window is broken/was broken/has been broken. (passive)

The form of the verb *be* used in the passive can change. The perfect participle always follows after, though. The passive can be used when a writer does not want the reader to know *who* performed the action of the verb. It is also useful when the subject of the verb is unimportant.

The driver drove the car expressed in the passive becomes *The car was driven*

4 Express the following sentences in the passive form.

 a *The stock broker bought the stocks.*

 b *I dropped your vase.*

 c *The pilot flew the prototype.*

How did I do?

I can vary participle use.

12: Persuasion

In this unit you will learn
- to examine aspects of persuasion

Get started

The following extract is from the beginning of an article that tries to persuade students to walk to school.

> Did you know that at least 700 million litres of petrol a week are wasted on unnecessary school runs? Nearly 20 per cent of students are overweight and our air pollution levels continue to rise. Anybody see a connection?
>
> You should walk to school. Yes ... I know it isn't always possible. It's often not at all possible. But it isn't always quite so impossible as people make out.

Statistics are important features of persuasive writing. They provide a factual basis for the claims that the writer makes. They form the scientific and mathematical evidence that the writer hopes will convince his or her readers.

Practice

1 a What statistic does the writer of the article use in connection with unnecessary school runs?

 b What statistic does she use about the weight of students?

 c What does the writer present as a fact without any statistical evidence?

Persuasive writing is a form that must engage fully with its readers. In other words it needs to speak convincingly and directly to those it wishes to persuade. One way of doing this is through **pronouns**.

2 Which single pronoun from the first sentence of the extract is used to appeal directly to the reader?

Another important way in which persuasive texts can engage is through the use of **rhetorical questions**. These are questions directed to the reader that are not intended to be answered.

3 Which two sentences in the passage are framed as rhetorical questions?

Persuasive writing needs to be energetic and engaged.

Modal verbs add meaning to the main verbs they modify. Look at the following examples.

You must *buy this new software*   (you have no choice – it's essential)

You should *buy this new software*   (it would be a very good idea)

You could *buy this new software*   (it's useful, but you can do without it)

In each case, the main verb (the infinitive *buy*) is modified by a different modal. The choice of modal alters the meaning each time.

4 What modal verb/main verb combination is used in the extract at the start of the second paragraph?

Notice how the writer avoids using a stronger modal verb. She doesn't want to be too pushy or her readers will be turned off.

The **passive form** is common in persuasive texts. *What* is done is often much more important than *who* has done it. Look at this example.

A million tonnes of rubbish is dumped every day.

The important thing (for this writer) is not *who* dumps the rubbish. It is *what* is dumped: a million tonnes of rubbish.

Read the passive sentence above again. A form of the verb *be* (in this case *is*) is combined with the perfect participle of the verb *dump*.

5 Look at the first sentence of the school run passage.

a Which form of the verb *be* is combined with which perfect participle?

b What does the writer want to draw attention to with this passive form?

c What does the use of the passive indicate the writer is not concerned about?

Revision booster

The writer of the school run article gives some direct advice at the beginning of the second paragraph. Her next sentence answers the objection this advice might raise. She actually writes *as if she has heard* the reader make the objection.

6 What single word does the writer use to suggest she has heard the reader's objection and is going to deal with it?

This is a great example of the way writers of persuasive texts can engage with their readers.

How did I do?

I know how to analyse aspects of persuasion.   ☑

13: Test 1

1 In the sentence, *Her tight shoes pinched horribly,* find a single example of each of the following

   a a noun

   b a verb

   c an adverb

   d an adjective

   e a determiner

2 Write down the five prepositions used in the following phrases.

Some red ants in the garden

The old nun with the wrinkled hand

That boy at the back

The crowd on the corner

These rickety bridges over the river

3 In the sentences that follow, identify

   a six noun phrases

   b three verbs

Some red ants built a large colony.

The wrinkled hand rocked her cradle.

That boy made an important statement.

4 **a** Identify the connective in each of the following sentences.

      He spoke angrily while the crowd pushed forward.

      I think we should go as it's not here.

      They don't know and they don't care.

   b In two of the above sentences the second clause (with the connective) can be moved to the front of a new sentence. Rewrite the two sentences in which the movement can take place.

5 In each of the following sentences, identify the verb (made up of one word or more) and then write down the tense of the verb. The first one has been done for you.

The uniformed soldier was driving a heavy truck.
was driving (past continuous)

   a It rains the whole time in this country.

   b I have tried so hard with this.

   c This set of computers is running at full capacity.

   d She had finished her work by then.

   e The goblet shattered.

6 **a** Each of the following sentences contains at least one adverbial phrase. One of the sentences contains two. Find all six.

The ball bounced over the hedge.

Our friends will arrive soon

Unfortunately, the pitch is waterlogged.

In a few moments, the concert will begin.

He blundered noisily through the undergrowth.

b Rewrite the second sentence by shifting the position of the adverb.

c Rewrite the fourth sentence by moving the adverbial phrase to the end of the clause.

7 In the sentences below, infinitive forms are used to create a persistent text, which is pushy and tries to be persuasive.

You should take a chance. Come with us. You must want to.

a Which are the three infinitive verbs in this text?

b Which modal verbs are used to intensify the persuasive appeal?

c Write out the sentence that begins with an imperative.

8 Think back to the descriptive technique of giving life and character to non-human objects. What is it called?

14: Combining clauses

In this unit you will learn
- to combine clauses

Get started

Recall that a **clause** is a part of a sentence that contains a verb. Writers can choose to produce single-clause sentences that look like these.

He howled in pain.

She drove the car.

It has snowed during the night.

I was happy at last.

You have finished it.

Steve agreed with her.

Practice

1. Identify the verb used in each of the single-clause sentences above. Remember that a verb can consist of a single word or a combination of words.

Remember also that single-clause sentences are only effective up to a point. All texts need sentences of more than one verb to create variety and depth. Verbs within sentences can be combined with the use of connectives. Look at this example.

Steve agreed with her. He understood her problem.

These two single-clause sentences could be combined in the following way with a connective.

Steve agreed with her because *he understood her problem.*

Of course, other connectives (such as *since, as soon as, when*) could be used to do the same job. Notice that the connective allows the writer to create a longer, more sophisticated sentence out of the pair of linked clauses.

Here are some more words used as connectives.

until   while   so   and   but   whenever   although   after

2. Look at the following pairs of clauses. Identify the connective that joins them in each case.

   a The baby cried whenever he was put down in his cot.

   b You must be careful or there could be trouble.

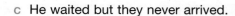

c He waited but they never arrived.

d You should go before they see you.

The continuous (or progressive) participle can also be used as a means of linking clauses. (The continuous participle is created by adding *ing* to the verb infinitive.) This is a very effective method, which you should use occasionally as a striking way of creating sentence variety.

Understanding her problem, Steve agreed with her.

3 Combine the following pairs of sentences, using continuous participles.

a Andre walked home. He felt miserable.

b The tears rolled down her cheeks. She laughed at her own joke.

c Everest is the world's highest mountain. It soars nearly 9000 metres into the sky.

> A variety of well-combined clauses produces mature and stylishly written sentences.

The past (or perfect) participle can also be used to link sentences. (The past participle is the form of the verb that follows *have/has* or *had* in the perfect tenses.)

This series has become very popular. It began only recently.

Begun only recently, this series has become very popular.

4 Combine the following pairs of sentences using the past participle as in the example above.

a The centre has been a success. It was completed last year.

b These mushrooms are delicious. They are cooked in butter.

c This is a beautiful necklace. It is encrusted with rubies.

Revision booster

For even greater variation, a participle phrase can sometimes be embedded after the first noun phrase in a sentence.

This necklace, encrusted with rubies, is beautiful.

Notice that the participle phrase embedded in the middle of the sentence is sectioned off with commas.

5 Rewrite the first two sentences from question 4 using the same method.

How did I do?

I can combine clauses. ☑

15: Reports

Get started

Read this extract from a report concerning the condition of an outdoor pool in a small Somerset town.

> Considering its age, the town's outdoor pool is in excellent condition. The linings have just been replaced and soon the pump room will be refitted. At the end of the year, work will begin on renovating the downstairs showers. Refurbished last in the early 1980s, these areas must be given attention.

Practice

1 a What area of the pool is about to be refitted?

   b When will work begin on the showers?

   c When were the showers last attended to?

This is a carefully written report that conveys detail efficiently and with good style. It demonstrates that one way of writing fluently is occasionally to use participle phrases at the beginning of sentences. This creates variety and is a good way of building sentences. Sentences that begin with participle phrases look as follows:

Shaking *its mane, the lion yawned.*   (starting with a continuous participle)

Published *in May, the book has sold well.*   (starting with a past participle)

Notice that these participle phrases are sectioned off with a comma, and that they should always relate to the subject of the verb.

2 In the extract above, which are the two participle phrases used at the start of sentences?

   a a continuous participle

   b a past participle

This report is largely concerned with *what* is being done *when*. Time relations can be indicated by writers through verb tense and choice of adverb. For example, the present perfect tense is used to describe actions recently completed.

3 a Which repair job has already been completed?

   b What adverb (a single word) is used to show that the repair happened very recently?

c Which verb tense is used to indicate the time of this recent repair?

d Which verb is added to the infinitives *be* and *begin* to indicate future time?

Look at these clauses.

The roads have been mended

The house has just been extended

The pipes will be relaid

All these clauses are **passive**. They are extremely common in reports and other forms of formal writing. They are an excellent way of communicating what needs to be done. They do not concern themselves with *who* will do it.

Read the clauses again. In none of them is the reader told *who* will do the mending, extending and relaying. This is not because the writer wishes to hide these details. It is because they are less important than the jobs to be done.

Notice the structure of these passive clauses.

noun phrase + form of the verb *be* + perfect participle

There are three passive clauses in the swimming pool text. The first one is

the linings have just been replaced   (the reader doesn't know who replaced them)

4 Write down the other two passive clauses.

> ❗ Use passives clauses to communicate a serious and efficient tone when needed.

Prefixes are letter units used at the beginnings of words that have common meanings. Here are some examples.

im	means *not*	e.g.	*impossible*	means	*not possible*
super	means *greater*	e.g.	*superpower*	means	*greater power*
pre	means *before*	e.g.	*prehistoric*	means	*before history*

5 What (two-letter) prefix meaning *again* is used at the start of four words in the passage?

Revision booster

Remember that modal verbs are used before infinitives to indicate things like probability, possibility and uncertainty.

6 Which individual modal verb is used in the final sentence of the passage to suggest obligation and urgency?

How did I do?

I know how to assess structure in reports.   ✔ ☐

16: Settings

Get started

Description can be a large (even the main) part of an imaginative text. Obviously, any creative writing must have some action, but it is not necessary to concentrate only on what happens (the events).

The following text concentrates largely on events.

> I walked slowly to the Head's office. I knocked nervously on the door. She told me to come in. She spoke to me angrily about what I'd done. Then she sent me back to class.

The text communicates a whole story in a few short sentences. It needs more **focus**.

The descriptive techniques used are limited. The description in the extract is based entirely on adverbs.

Practice

1   Which adverb is used to describe how

a   the narrator (the storyteller) walked to the office?

b   the narrator knocked on the door?

c   the Head spoke to the narrator?

> **!**   Even when you want to include a lot of action, do not forget the importance of description.

Adverbs can only do part of the job, though. A piece of writing like the one above needs more description to be really effective. There is too much action and not enough focus on detail. The following description zooms in a little more.

> I walked slowly to the Head's office and saw a single wooden chair just outside the door. I sat down. It was cold and hard.

There are two additional main verbs here, *saw* and *sat*. The action, however, is now fading into the background. The description is more important.

2   a   What four-word noun phrase is used to describe the chair?

b   How many chairs have been made available?

c   Why might the number of chairs available be important?

d   What two adjectives are used to describe the chair?

Notice that the description is funnelling the reader towards an understanding of the narrator's feelings. This is what is interesting in the text.

3 a Look again at the adverb in the first sentence. What does it suggest about the narrator's feelings?

   b Consider the adjectives used to describe the chair. How are these used to suggest the narrator's own feelings at this point?

The adverbs, noun phrases and adjectives used in this sort of description are essential to the mood of the text. To see how this works, take the adverb *busily*, the noun phrase *an armchair* and two adjectives *warm* and *cosy*. If these are used instead of their equivalents in the second of the texts, the description becomes like this.

I walked busily to the Head's office and saw an armchair just outside the door. I sat down. It was warm and cosy.

So you can see that the reason for describing a setting in detail may actually be *to suggest the narrator's feelings.*

Once you get used to writing descriptions, you'll find that you can add layers of detail that continue to suggest *feelings*. Remember that it is usually a narrator's feelings and emotions that make imaginative texts interesting to an audience. The second text could be continued in the following way.

> I walked slowly to the Head's office and saw a single wooden chair just outside the door. I sat down. It was cold and hard. I shuffled uncomfortably. The light was glaring and harsh. On the wall opposite was a mask, part of a Year 7 display. It seemed to grin at me mockingly.

Which two infinitives are used at the start of imperative sentences in this extract?

4 a What verb is used to suggest awkward and uncomfortable movement in the seat?

   b What two adjectives describe the light?

   c What does the mask seem to be doing to the narrator?

Notice how, in this new text, the narrator hasn't yet even knocked on the Head's door. Lots of detail and emotion is communicated *without* the need for lots of action.

How did I do?

I can construct imaginative settings. ☑

17: Perspective

In this unit you will learn
▶ to consider perspective

Get started

Much of what we read on a daily basis is written by people who need to grab our attention. They do this by writing with attitude. They adopt a **perspective** (a viewpoint or an angle) on current events and try to express it with colour and force.

Read the following example of this from the start of a well-known newspaper column.

> *Reality TV is mental junk food. Can't be bothered to cook tonight? Go to the takeaway. Can't be bothered to think? Watch Big Brother.*

Remember that writers often need to grab a reader's attention quickly. Otherwise the reader might pick up something else to look at. A good way of doing this is through a punchy metaphor, a quickfire comparison of one thing with another.

It is obvious that cigarettes are just replacement dummies.

Our love for celebrity is the new religion.

Charlotte's work is a wall that she hides behind.

In the third example, Charlotte's work is compared to a wall. People can hide behind walls. Charlotte hides behind her work *as if it were* a wall.

Practice

1. a What two things are compared in the first of the three sentences above?

   b The metaphor about dummies reveals the writer's viewpoint: what is it?

2. a Which two things are compared at the start of the article above?

   b What is the writer's view of both things being compared?

The writer sets up an imaginary conversation with the reader. She asks questions and then provides answers.

3. a What is the writer's first question?

   b The reader cannot give an answer to her question so the writer assumes one. What does she assume it is?

4 Look again at this first question. Help rephrase it by thinking of an adjective that would fill the blank space in the following sentence.

Are you too _____ to cook tonight?

5 Summarise what you now know about the writer's views on reality TV and the people who watch it.

Remember that a writer's angle is just that – an angle. A writer's view is an opinion that may or may not be sensible. As a thoughtful reader, your task is to recognise *what* is expressed and *how* it is done. Then you need to make your own mind up.

The column about reality TV continues like this.

> The term 'reality' is, of course, complete nonsense. The contestants on these shows are just actors without scripts.

Writers have various ways in which they can make their viewpoints more convincing. One of them is through the selective use of short adverbial phrases like these.

no doubt

for certain

without doubt

They appear in sentences, sectioned off with commas.

She is, without doubt, the most excellent actress of her generation.

The adverbial phrase is used to strengthen the statement in which the writer believes. It in no way makes the statement true.

Notice, as in many cases, that an adverbial can be replaced with a single adverb.

She is certainly/definitely/clearly the most excellent actress of her generation.

6 a What (two-word) adverbial phrase is used by the writer of the reality TV text?

b What adjective (meaning *total* or *absolute*) is also used to strengthen the statement?

Revision booster

Writers often use single quotation marks to sneer or laugh at things they don't like. It is as if to say, *Some people might think this, but I don't.*

7 a Which word does the writer sneer at like this in her text?

b What suggestion does she seem to be making about reality TV?

This can be an effective technique if it is used in moderation.

How did I do?

I know how to consider perspective. ☐

18: Speech in literature

In this unit you will learn
▶ to analyse speech in a classic text

Get started

Read this passage from *The Yellow Wallpaper,* an extraordinary short story by a writer called Charlotte Perkins Gilman. It is an account of a woman, told in her own words, who is slowly going mad. One of the symptoms of her madness is that she believes there is a female prisoner behind the patterned wallpaper in her bedroom. In this scene, she wakes up in the middle of the night with her husband, John, beside her.

> John was asleep and I hated to waken him, so I kept still and watched the moonlight on that undulating wallpaper till I felt creepy.
>
> The faint figure behind seemed to shake the pattern, just as if she wanted to get out.
>
> I got up softly and went to feel and see if the paper did move, and when I came back John was awake.
>
> "What is it little girl?" he said. "Don't go walking about like that – you'll get cold."
>
> I thought it was a good time to talk, so I told him that I was not gaining here, and that I wished he would take me away.
>
> "Why darling!" said he. "Our lease will be up in three weeks, and I can't see how to leave before."

Practice

1 The narrator (the woman slowly going mad) is childlike.

   a Which word at the end of the first sentence seems a little childlike?

   b Which (two-word) noun phrase suggests that her husband views her as a child?

Structures can be childlike, as well as vocabulary. Look at the following example.

"Can I have my present yet?" I asked Daddy.

"Not yet," replied he.

The word *Daddy* is nowadays seen as childlike. The word order *replied he* is also childlike.

2 a Write out these two words (*replied he*) in their usual order.

   b Where might you find a structure like this?

   c Write out the example of this structure used in the passage above.

3 What verb does the narrator use to describe the actions of the figure behind the wallpaper pattern?

Remember *imagery,* the art of creating a picture in a reader's mind.

4 What picture is suggested by the verb you identified in question 3?

5 The narrator has a childlike fascination in what she thinks she sees. What does she do that proves she is *certain* she saw *something* in the wallpaper?

 Read the whole of *The Yellow Wallpaper*. It is a breathtaking and terrifying account of a woman's descent into madness.

The conversation between the narrator and her husband continues like this.

> "I don't weigh a bit more," said I, "nor as much; and my appetite may be better in the evening when you are here but it is worse in the morning when you are away!"
>
> "Bless her little heart," said he with a big hug. "She shall be as sick as she pleases … Really, dear, you are better!"
>
> "Better in body, perhaps –" I began …

Younger (and sometimes older) children often try hard to avoid upsetting or disturbing their parents. The narrator is like this with her husband.

6 What does she try to avoid doing to John at the start of the first passage?

7 In this passage, the reader learns that she does something only when John is there. What does the narrator do properly only when her husband is with her?

She avoids finishing her sentence at the end of this passage to avoid upsetting John.

8 What was she about to say that would have upset her husband?

Revision booster

John uses the determiner *her* and the pronoun *she.*

9 a What is so odd about using these two words *in this situation*?

  b In which situations might it be normal for people to use language like this?

How did I do?

I can analyse speech in a classic text.

19: Phrases and clauses

In this unit you will learn
▶ to express detail concisely

Get started

Remember that a clause is a part of a sentence that contains a verb.

the man   is a noun phrase without a verb

the man in the film is a pair of noun phrases linked by a preposition

the man walked   is a clause (because it includes a verb, *walked*)

Practice

1 Which of the following are phrases (or pairs of phrases) and which are clauses?

a *some people at the stall*

b *she drives*

c *a couple*

d *the angry elephant roared*

e *my friend*

f *accidents happen*

Noun phrases can be made up of a single noun or pronoun. They can also be formed from clusters of determiners, adjectives and nouns

it   (single pronoun)

Gabriel   (single noun)

that green parrot   (determiner + adjective + noun)

*that green parrot with
the blue wings*   (two noun phrases linked by a preposition)

2 Look back at the phrases and clauses in question 1 and identify a noun phrase made up of

a a pronoun

b a single noun

c a determiner plus an adjective plus a noun

3 Which of the phrases in question 1 consists of a pair of noun phrases joined by a preposition?

Extended noun phrases need to be used in sentences of more than a single clause. Look at the following example.

It was a beautiful tree. It produced colourful, sweet-scented blossom every year.

Both sentences contain extended noun phrases.

a beautiful tree and *colourful, sweet-scented blossom*

The detail is very good, but it could be expressed with greater economy. It could be more concise and more focused. This can be achieved by communicating the description in a single sentence.

It was a beautiful tree, which produced colourful, sweet-scented blossom every year.

Notice that *which* is used as a connective to join the two original sentences. It *refers back* to the tree that starts the description. For that reason, it is called a **relative pronoun**. Here is a list of the four common relative pronouns.

who   which   whose   that

Notice the following points. The connective *who* refers to people. The connective *whose* refers to something belonging to the original noun. The connectives *which* and *that* refer to things and are often interchangeable.

Extended noun phrases are an excellent way of expressing detail concisely. In other words, a good deal of information can be packed into noun phrases and this produces pacier, more interesting texts. Using well-developed noun phrases in a selective way will improve your writing style.

4 Join the following pairs of sentences using one of the connectives above. Use the example about the tree as your guide.

a *The old lady was a happy person. She made friends easily.*

b *It is a big problem. It causes lots of disagreements.*

c *Think about these people. Their lives have been changed.*

Revision booster

Increased variety can be achieved by embedding the second (or subordinate) clause within the main clause.

The old lady, who made friends easily, was a happy person.

5 Join the following pair of short sentences using an appropriate connective. Then embed the subordinate clause within the main clause following the example above.

The alien was a thoughtful being. He always helped others.

How did I do?

I know how to express detail concisely.

20: Promotional writing

In this unit you will learn
▷ to explore promotional writing

Get started

Read the text that follows. It is designed to promote a housing development.

> Shoebury sits proudly at the head of the Thames estuary. For centuries, she has welcomed visitors to these islands. In more recent times, the town has had a crucial role in our defence against invaders. During the middle of the Victorian era, a mighty garrison was settled. The soldiers have left now, but their superb buildings remain.

Practice

1 a Where exactly is Shoebury?

b When was the garrison first settled?

c What is left of the garrison?

Promotional writing attempts to be as positive as it can possibly be about what it describes. It needs, after all, to have a very direct impact on its readership. All promotional writing, at some point, aims to convince a reader that its advertised product is worth buying.

2 In the first sentence of the text,

a what verb is used to suggest calm and dignity?

b what adverb suggests that Shoebury can boast about its position?

Estuaries are often (metaphorically) described as the *mouths* of rivers.

3 a What metaphor is used to describe the position on the Thames estuary?

b Why do you think this metaphor was chosen?

Personal pronouns are used to refer to nouns. Look at the following examples.

(she/her) the woman   *(they/them) these builders*   *(it) this stone*

Notice that, as a very common rule, people are referred to by the pronouns *he* and *she*. *Things* are referred to by the pronoun *it*.

Shoebury, like a stone, is a *thing*.

4 a What pronoun is used to refer to Shoebury in the second sentence?

b What is the effect of this pronoun?

c What other non-living thing is sometimes referred to by this pronoun?

Three-word noun phrases are a common descriptive technique. They consist of a determiner, an adjective and a noun. Look at the following examples.

these great towers

this tremendous idea

a stunning conclusion

5 Three noun phrases, identical in structure to those above, appear in the text. They have been carefully constructed to suggest the importance of Shoebury and the soldiers who once lived there.

a Which noun phrase indicates the vital part played by the town in stopping invaders?

b Which noun phrase suggests the great power of the garrison?

c Which noun phrase is used to describe the wonderful architecture still standing?

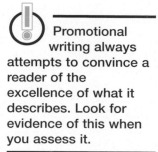

Promotional writing always attempts to convince a reader of the excellence of what it describes. Look for evidence of this when you assess it.

Look at the start of the second, third and fourth sentences of the text. They all begin with adverbial phrases that are sectioned off with commas. These adverbial phrases all tell the reader *when* things occurred. Like adverbs, adverbial phrases can often be moved around in sentences to create different effects. Consider the following example.

For millions of years, dinosaurs ruled the Earth.

Dinosaurs ruled the Earth for millions of years.

6 a Rewrite the second sentence in the passage with the adverbial phrase moved to the end.

b Repeat this process for the third and fourth sentences.

Now read the whole of the rewritten text to yourself. It should still make good sense but notice how the style has been damaged by moving the adverbial phrases. The text will now seem much more like a list. Remember this effect in your own writing.

Revision booster

This promotional text is anxious to establish that Shoebury has a long and distinguished history. Evidence of a dignified history is often important for something that is new, such as a housing development.

7 a Which two-word phrase describes Shoebury's importance over hundreds of years?

b Which phrase recalls an important period in British history?

How did I do?

I know how to explore promotional writing.   ☐

21: Features of narrative

In this unit you will learn
▸ to study features of narrative

Get started

Recently, a school at Carmarthen in Wales had an open evening to which visitors were welcomed. Nick Evans, a Year 9 student, was in charge of greeting the guests as they arrived. After the event, he was asked to write up an account of his experiences on the school website. This is how it starts.

The evening began very smoothly. The most popular attraction in the entire hall was the line of display boards that demonstrated progression from Year 7 to Year 13. They were arranged, like dominoes, so that guests could move gradually up the age range as they walked. It was also a pleasure to see so many younger brothers and sisters at the evening. While Mrs Jones, Head of Upper School, was speaking, some of these younger siblings hid behind our display boards. One of them decided to see what would happen if he pushed the Year 7 board. It crashed into Year 8, which then knocked down Year 9. This went on all the way up to Year 13. Seven years of work destroyed in two seconds!

Practice

1 Look closely at Nick's first sentence.

   a Which verb does he use to emphasise the success of the start of the evening?

   b Which adverb emphasises this efficiency and ease?

   c Certain adverbs *intensify* other adverbs. They make the original adverb stronger. Which adverb is used like this in Nick's writing?

2 Now replace the verb you identified in the first sentence with a new verb *went*.

   a Contrast the effect of this new verb with the one chosen by Nick.

   b What reasons do you think Nick had for his choice of verb?

Remember that large amounts of information can be communicated clearly and efficiently through expanded noun phrases. This happens in the second sentence of Nick's account.

3 a Which eight-word noun phrase does Nick use before the verb in his second sentence?

   b In the same sentence, which five-word noun phrase does the relative pronoun *that* refer to?

Recall the term *cohesion.* It is used as a term to describe the way texts hold (or *stick*) together. Cohesive texts can refer forwards to future events or backwards to things that are past. They often do both of these things.

You have already identified an example of cohesion by looking at Nick's choice of verb in the first sentence. It directs the reader (it *looks forward*) to a time in the text when things aren't so smooth.

4 Which single noun in the third sentence, sectioned off with another word in commas, prepares the reader for what later happens to the display boards?

⚠ Expanded noun phrases and the use of relative pronouns are excellent ways of expressing lots of detail. The second sentence of the extract is a good example of this.

In the fourth sentence, the reader is introduced to the *agents* of the later destruction. At this point in the text, there doesn't seem much point in mentioning them. Their importance becomes important only later.

5 Which seemingly unimportant people are introduced in the fourth sentence?

Reference chains are another cohesive device. These are chains of noun phrases that run through a text, making reference to the same thing. They can also be used as a way of focusing in from the general to the particular. Look at this example.

Many people like fast food. Some people eat a lot. This man eats ten burgers a day.

The noun reference chain goes from *many people* to *some people* to *this man.*

6 Write down the noun reference chain that Nick uses to focus in on the agents of the accident.

Revision booster

Jokey exaggeration can also form a useful part of this sort of narrative. Nick uses the technique at the end of this extract.

7 a How does the writer use exaggeration at the end of the passage?
   b How does he use punctuation to signal his joke?

How did I do?

I can study features of narrative. ☑

22: Character in fiction

In this unit you will learn
▶ to create character in fiction

Get started

Writers have a few basic means of describing the characters they choose to place in their texts.

● They can refer to them neutrally with pronouns and nouns.

He lived next door.

Mrs Thorpe was 29 years old.

● Writers can develop character, if they wish, by using adjectives.

Mrs Thorpe was happy.

● Writers can also *reveal* character by describing what people actually *do*.

He slipped quietly through the door.

Practice

1 a What verb and adverb combination is used to describe the character's actions in the last sentence above?

b What *might* these actions reveal about the personality and situation of this character?

In your own writing, you should use all of these different ways of referring to character. It is the last way, though, that most students need to practise. Character that is *revealed* is much more interesting and much closer to real life. Read the following passage.

> The sick man lay still on the bed. Jonah looked tenderly down at him. Every few moments, he moistened the flannel and bathed his brother's forehead. When he was sure his patient slept, he slipped quietly through the door.

2 Look at the second sentence of the passage.

a What adverb is used to describe the way Jonah acts?

b What is Jonah actually doing for his brother?

c Why does he slip quietly through the door?

3 Compare your last answer with the one you gave to the similar question in 1b. It is almost certainly different, perhaps very different. What has caused your answer to change?

If you were asked to sum up Jonah's character in sentences containing adjectives, you would probably arrive at this sort of thing.

Jonah was kind.

Jonah was tender.

There is a place for sentences like these. It is preferable on most occasions, however, to give readers the evidence and let them come to their own conclusions. Your own fictional style will improve (as will your marks) if you use the approach used above.

Read the following vivid character description.

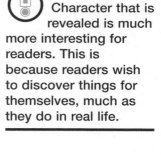

Character that is revealed is much more interesting for readers. This is because readers wish to discover things for themselves, much as they do in real life.

> I sat trembling as Humbert's balloon face leered up at me. At first, his mouth was closed in a thin line and his eyes were narrowed. He looked at me silently and with total contempt. His nose seemed to wrinkle up in disgust at my very presence. Suddenly his mouth opened to reveal uneven yellow teeth and an enormous pink tongue. He shouted abuse, and as he did so, covered me in flecks of spit.

Characterisation is the art of creating fictional character. The *narrator* is hardly characterised here at all except by the use of a single adjective.

4 Which adjective is used to characterise the narrator and show his fear?

Humbert is characterised in detail. This is mainly done through his facial features.

5 How are the following of Humbert's features described?

a face

b eyes

c teeth

6 Which other of Humbert's facial features are also described?

7 What unpleasant *physical* thing happens to the narrator at the end of the extract?

Revision booster

Based on the evidence *revealed* in the passage above, it is unlikely that you would write the following adjectival statement about Humbert.

Humbert was a kind and attractive man.

8 What would you write?

Note how much less effective such statements are than those that *reveal* character through a description of behaviour.

How did I do?

I can create character in fiction. ☐

23: Instructions and advice

In this unit you will learn
- to analyse instructions and advice

Get started

Read the following text that provides instructions for making a kind of specialist coffee.

> Heat the water until it reaches boiling point. Actually, the perfect temperature is 96 degrees, but most people cannot measure the temperature of hot water that accurately. If you boil the water and let it cool down for a few minutes then the temperature of the water will be fine. It's what I always do and it always seems to work.

Imperative sentences are formed using the infinitive form of the verb, without a subject. They look like this.

Take an aspirin.

Be careful while you are walking there.

Stay close to the shore.

In the second sentence you can see there is an understood modal verb: *You should be careful*. This imperative form is very useful for giving advice and instructions. This is because the action of the sentence (communicated by the verb) is more important than the subject of the action (which is *you*). The fact that the sentence is addressed to *you* is assumed.

Practice

1 Write out the sentence in the passage that uses the imperative form.

2 a Find the five-word phrase later on in the passage that begins with the connective *if*.

   b Turn this five-word phrase into a three-word imperative clause.

Read this new sentence through to yourself, and note how the tone has been changed.

Look at the single-word adverb at the start of the second sentence. This adverb is a *cohesive* device. It refers *back* to the previous instruction and *forward* to the comment that follows.

3 a What does the adverb suggest about the instruction in the first sentence?

   b What does the adverb promise in the sentence to come?

   c Why can the advice of the second sentence not be followed by most people?

Adverbs placed at the start of sentences are usually sectioned off by punctuation.

4 What punctuation is used to section off adverbs at the start of sentences?

Recall that adverbs can often by replaced by adverbial phrases. Adverbial phrases are phrases (two words or more in length) that function in the same way as single-word adverbs. Look at the following example.

particularly   can be replaced by the two-word adverbial   *in particular*

5 Look again at the adverb that starts the second sentence of the text. It can be replaced by either two- or three-word adverbial phrases. Write down the adverbial phrases that could replace this single-word adverb.

Advice and information often contain statements called *if ... then* clauses. These are clauses that tell the reader *what will happen* should certain conditions be fulfilled. Look at this example.

If *the tyres are looked after well* then *they will last for years.*

In this example, the condition to be fulfilled is that the tyres are looked after well.

6 What will happen if the condition in this example is fulfilled?

This is an important feature of advice for the following reason. Many readers will not follow instructions (perhaps wisely) unless they are provided with a good reason for doing so. *If ... then* clauses show readers the consequences of following (and not following) advice.

7 Locate the *if ... then* clause in the extract about the coffee. What will happen if the reader fulfils the conditions given in the advice?

If ... then clauses are commonly used as threats. *If* you don't do as I say *then* this will happen. Looked at in this way, you could easily consider a threat as one of the strongest forms of advice!

Revision booster

Information can be tedious to read.

8 How does the writer of the coffee text try to introduce more interest at the end of the passage?

How did I do?

I know how to analyse instructions and advice. ☐

24: Spelling errors

In this unit you will learn
▶ to spell commonly confused words

Get started

Often words are misspelled because they become confused with other words. Perhaps the most common example of this is in the two high frequency words *quite* and *quiet.* Looking at the grammar of these words will help to pull them apart.

● *quite* is an adverb that means something like the adverb *fairly.* It normally suggests that although something isn't brilliant, it isn't bad either.

   The new software is quite *good.*

● *quiet* is an adjective that describes a noun.

   It was a very quiet *evening by the sea.*

● *quietly* is an adverb that describes the action of doing something without noise.

   He whispered quietly *to himself in the corner.*

Practice

1 Read the following sentences. Identify the correct choice of word in each case.

   a The mouse was extremely *quite/quiet/quietly.*

   b He wanted to have a *quite/quiet/quietly* day by the sea.

   c The wind whispered *quite/quiet/quietly* in the trees.

   d The road is *quite/quiet/quietly* a long way from the track.

   e It's going to be *quite/quiet/quietly* a long time before then.

Your knowledge of grammar can also help you with another commonly misspelled word, *already.* This is an adverb that means something has happened.

I have already *spoken to her.*

Already is one of a group of words that begins with the letters *al.*

although   almost   altogether   alright   always

These words can *never* be spelled in the following ways.

allready   allthough   allmost   alltogether   allright   allways

Sometimes the word *all* can be used before words like *ready* and *right* and *ways*. When it is used like this it means *every* or *everyone* or *everything*.

Is the team all *ready?*   *Is everyone ready?*

Are the fireworks all *ready?*   *Is everything ready?*

Are all *ways blocked?*   *Is every way blocked?*

Notice, though, that the word *all* remains separate from the word that follows it.

Use your knowledge of grammar to help improve your spelling.

The following pairs of words are very often confused.

practice/practise   device/devise   advice/advise

The first word in each pair (the one with the letter *c*) is an abstract noun. The second word in each pair (the one with the letter *s*) is a verb. You can *hear* the difference in the second two pairs. The noun is used to describe a thing.

My *advice* is to go to the gym.

With enough *practice* you will improve.

The verb is used to describe the act of doing something.

I *practised* for hours.

She is *advising* him on his finances.

He *devises* ways of improving road safety.

He will *practise* until he gets better.

② The following sentences contain some of the common mistakes looked at in this unit. Locate each error and write down the corrected version. You should be able to find ten mistakes in all.

He practices the guitar for allmost all of his spare time.

All though it is quite by the river it is still fairly busy.

My advise to anyone in this business is to be ready for anything.

Is the building allready complete? They've worked quiet quickly on it.

The buildings are already. They worked on them for allmost a year.

Allthough it's a long way away, we arrived quite early.

How did I do?

I know how to spell commonly confused words.

25: Metaphor in Shakespeare

> In this unit you will learn
> ▶ to look at metaphor in Shakespeare

Get started

Read the following lines from Shakespeare's play, *As You Like It*. They are from the beginning of a speech made by a character called Jaques. He is reflecting on the nature of progress through life.

> All the world's a stage,
> And all the men and women merely players: [players – actors]
> They have their exits and their entrances;
> And one man in his time plays many parts,
> His acts being seven ages.

Remember that a metaphor is a comparison between different things. Metaphors can be expressed as follows.

India is a precious jewel.

The country is compared to a jewel. The comparison emphasises the preciousness and beauty of India. Sometimes metaphors can be extended.

India is a precious jewel with many faces.

The metaphor suggests that just as a cut jewel can have many sides, so India too has many different aspects.

Practice

 a What metaphor in the extract above does Jaques use to describe the world?

b How does Jaques extend the metaphor to include living men and women?

c Jaques uses a metaphor to divide up people's lives, just as a play is divided up. What are the natural time divisions in people's lives compared to?

Read how Jaques describes the first two ages through which we live.

> At first the infant,
> Mewling and puking in the nurse's arms.
> And then the whining school-boy, with his satchel
> And shining morning face, creeping like snail
> Unwillingly to school.

Jaques suggests these first two ages are not very attractive.

2 What dominates the first of these ages?

3 a Which (single-word) verb describes the way the schoolboy walks to school?

   b How is his movement made to seem slow?

4 Everything suggests that the schoolboy is miserable except for the adjective *shining*. How do you explain the fact that the schoolboy's face is shining?

Jaques then goes on to describe the third and fourth ages.

> And then the lover,
> Sighing like furnace, with a woeful ballad   [ballad – love song]
> Made to his mistress' eyebrow. Then a soldier,
> Full of strange oaths and bearded like the pard,   [pard – leopard]
> Jealous in honour, sudden and quick in quarrel,
> Seeking the bubble reputation
> Even in the cannon's mouth.

 Find a copy of this speech and read Jaques' comments about the final three ages.

5 How are the lover's sighs made to seem passionate and fiery?

6 Lovers have often been teased for praising *everything* about the person they love. How are the songs of this particular lover made to seem a bit ridiculous?

Revision booster

7 Beards were an important sign of maturity in Shakespeare's day. How is a full beard made to seem an object of worth?

8 Soldiers are concerned about their reputations *even in the cannon's mouth.* What does Shakespeare mean by this?

9 Shakespeare suggests that reputation can disappear immediately. What noun (used here as an adjective) suggests that reputation is fragile?

How did I do?

I can look at metaphor in Shakespeare.   ✔ ☐

1 Remember that the continuous (or present) participle is the *ing* form of the verb. The perfect (or past) participle combines with a form of the verb *have* to make the perfect tenses.

For each of the following verbs, write down

a the continuous participle

b the perfect participle

be   make   go   sleep   surprise

2 If a verb ends in the letter *e* what happens to it in the *ing* spelling?

3 Sometimes, participles can do the job of connectives in joining separate clauses. Look at the following example.

I sat up suddenly. The noise woke me.

Woken by the noise, I sat up suddenly.

Make single sentences out of the following clauses using *either* the continuous *or* the perfect participle from the verb in the second clause.

a I cried out. I was troubled in mind.

b He walked away. He laughed to himself.

c We ate our food. We felt content.

d The room was silent. Dust covered it.

4 Read the following extract.

> Did you know that 73 per cent of children are at 'severe risk' from tooth decay? Something must be done about this. Help us solve the problem before it is too late.

a What is the name of the sort of question that forms the first sentence?

b What is used in the first half of this sentence to support the writer's argument?

c What is used in the second half of the sentence for a similar purpose?

d Write down the modal verb used for emphasis in the second sentence.

e The last sentence begins with an infinitive. What are sentences like this called?

f What kind of writing would you say this extract comes from?

5 Look at this pair of sentences.

Cows are producing milk in record quantities.

Milk is being produced in record quantities.

    a What has disappeared from the second sentence?

    b Why, in this case, is it not needed?

    c What is the name for sentences like this?

6 Transform the following sentences in the same way as the example in question 5.

    a Farmers grow corn in the summer.

    b Miners mine gold in South Africa.

    c The government advised us to stop.

7 Read the following text.

> Stevens barked angrily at the retreating boys. In the rush, he had forgotten his keys. He looked down bitterly at the splatters of mud on his shiny new shoes.

    a Write down two adverbs that suggest Stevens' anger and disappointment.

    b The verb used in the first sentence is used as a metaphor. What is this verb?

    c What does the verb cause Stevens to be compared to?

    d What is the name for the three-word phrase at the beginning of the second sentence?

    e Look at the noun phrase at the end of the extract. It begins with the determiner *the*. How many prepositions are used to link the different parts of this noun phrase? What are they?

    f Why are noun phrases like this useful?

8 Link the following clauses using either *who* or *which* or *whose*.

    a It is a major issue. It creates a lot of problems.

    b He is a happy animal. He loves playing with children.

    c This is the injured student. Her bravery was so impressive.

    d It is a fantastic place. It reminds me of great times.

    e Come and look at the tree. Its roots are causing problems.

Answers

1 Phrases in sentences

1   The answers should be similar to these: *sugar, the sugar, the brown sugar, some sweet sugar*
2   *the eagle, the unlucky rabbit, Mr Aggarwal, the airship, bright stones, the beach*
3   a   *the baby, mud, many insects, complicated homes, large planes, serious pollution*
    b   *eats, build, cause*
4   a   NP + verb + NP + connective + NP + verb
    b   NP + verb + connective + NP + verb
    c   NP + verb + NP + connective + NP + verb + NP
5   *Amit dances, his brother sings, Jana did the shopping, Freddy left school*
6   a   *As the army entered, the city fell.*
    b   *Before the rabbit could escape, the eagle swooped.*
    c   *If there's no other way through, dig a hole.*
    d   *Until she arrives, I can't leave.*

2 Noun phrases

1   There are many possible answers. The nouns should be similar to these: *people, car, clothes, window, house*
2   a   *many, a, these, that, the*
    b   *rusty, new, broken, cold*
3   a   *behind*
    b   *on*
    c   *with*
    d   *at*
    e   *of*
4   a   *he*
    b   *that old suit of armour*
    c   *good ideas*
    d   *the man with the loud voice*
    e   *the shadows*
5   There are many possible answers. The verbs should be similar to these:
    a   *cried*
    b   *spoke*
    c   *rang*

3 Structuring information

1   *Hercules, the name of the Roman emperor*
2   *from ancient Greek*
3   a   The word *Tyrannosaurus* comes from ancient Greek.
    b   It was discovered over one hundred years ago.
4   The size of a Tyrannosaurus' head is compared to a fully grown human. The height is compared to a double decker bus.
5   *Tyrannosaurus, tyrant lizard, this great dinosaur, T Rex, this extraordinary beast, a true giant, a fearful predator*

4 Verb forms

1   a   *my youngest daughter, that valuable gold necklace, we*
    b   *swims, disappeared, arrived*
2   a   *she throws, she threw, she is throwing, she has thrown*
    b   *she plays, she played, she is playing, she has played*
    c   *she sings, she sang, she is singing, she has sung*
3   a   *It, the old black sheep, most younger people, that broken cistern in the toilet, he, the man in the dark glasses*
    b   *hurts, is limping, have stopped, has emptied, is teething, waited*

5 Using adverbs

1   *crept, work, broke, are eating, sank*
2   a   *with great speed*
    b   *to their house*
    c   *in ten minutes*
3   The adverbs should be similar to these: *fast/quickly/speedily, there/home, soon/later/next*
4   *The pool quickly emptied. Quickly, the pool emptied.*

6 Locating detail

1   a   *at noon*
    b   *behind Smith Street*
    c   *by mid-afternoon*
2   a   *officially*
    b   *gradually*
    c   *progress* (or *will progress*)
3   *The carnival begins officially; Officially, the carnival begins*
4   *at noon*
5   *in the town square, beside the library*
6   *The procession will reach the park by mid-afternoon.*
7   *will leave, will progress, will reach*
8   *begins*

7 Parts of verbs

1   a   *laugh*
    b   *smile*
    c   *try*
    d   *write*
    e   *eat*
2   a   *no*
    b   *yes*
    c   *yes*
    d   *yes*
3   a   *am, are, were*
    b   *be, have, mix*
4   a   *have, has, had*
    b   *make, arrive, break*

8 Biography

1 a the rain
   b *flood*
2 a *smiling from ear to ear*
   b The reader immediately gets the impression that he is a friendly, welcoming sort of character.
3 a The first and the second paragraphs both refer to rain.
   b The second paragraph moves the subject matter on by referring to the rain in Malaya.
4 This detail suggests that perhaps William Brown is living a little in the past. Maybe he is unwilling to move along with the times.
5 a cricket
   b It suggests he was living a traditional life, playing traditional colonial games.
6 a *is raining, is smiling*
   b *arrive, knock, welcomes*
7 a *have had, have done*
   b *had lived, had improved*
   c *was playing, was staying*

9 Infinitives

1 a *will*
   b This modal verb has the effect of making the verb express future time. (It can also suggest an order.)
2 a The modal *must* has the stronger impact.
   b *will, shall*
3 The preposition *to* needs to go between *ought* and an infinitive.
4 a There are lots of possible answers. The answer should be similar to this: *Could he come to our house?*
   b The subject moves between the modal and the main verb.
5 *Turn on the oven.*
6 *Clear, Help*
7 a *can*
   b *must*
   c *would*

10 Creating effects

1 a *the mean wind*
   b A miserable cold mood is created, as if the wind has some spiteful desire to get the man on the moor.
2 a *blew*
   b *chillingly*
3 His eyes are blurred because the cold wind is making them water.
4 a He uses *st* and *k* sounds.
   b A harsh and cold effect is created by these sounds.
5 The trees are compared to *naked, broken scarecrows.*

6 a This suggests the trees do not have leaves.
   b *naked*
7 The most obvious way of rewriting this sentence is *And then I saw the light.* It is not as dramatic as the verbless sentence.

11 Using participles

1 a *thought*
   b *stayed*
   c *made*
   d *had*
   e *brought*
   f *taken*
2 a *I have bought stuff online.*
   b *We have eaten snails.*
   c *They have left.*
3 a *the dried earth*
   b *these fallen civilisations*
   c *the ripened grapes*
4 a *The stocks were/have been bought.*
   b *Your vase was/has been dropped.*
   c *The prototype was/has been flown.*

12 Persuasion

1 a The writer says that at least 700 million litres of petrol a week are wasted on unnecessary school runs.
   b She says that nearly 20 per cent of students are overweight.
   c She says that air pollution levels continue to rise but does not supply the figures.
2 *you*
3 The first and third sentences are framed as rhetorical questions.
4 *should walk*
5 a *are wasted*
   b She wants to draw attention to the amount of petrol that is wasted.
   c The writer is not (in this sentence) concerned about who is using this petrol.
6 *yes*

13 Test 1

1 a *shoes*
   b *pinched*
   c *horribly*
   d *tight*
   e *Her*
2 *in, with, at, on, over*
3 a *some red ants, a large colony, the wrinkled hand, her cradle, that boy, an important statement*
   b *built, rocked, made*
4 a *while, as, and*
   b *While the crowd pushed forward, he spoke angrily. As it's not here, I think we should go.*

5   a   *rains* (present)
    b   *have tried* (present perfect)
    c   *is running* (present continuous)
    d   *had finished* (past perfect)
    e   *shattered* (past)
6   a   *over the hedge, soon, unfortunately, in a few moments, noisily, through the undergrowth*
    b   *Our friends will soon arrive. Soon, our friends will arrive.*
    c   *The concert will begin in a few moments.*
7   a   *take, come, want*
    b   *should, must*
    c   *Come with us.*
8   personification

14 Combining clauses

1   *howled, drove, has snowed, was, have finished, agreed*
2   a   *whenever*
    b   *or*
    c   *but*
    d   *before*
3   a   *Feeling miserable, Andre walked home. /Walking home, Andre felt miserable.*
    b   *Laughing at her own joke, the tears rolled down her cheeks./The tears rolling down her cheeks, she laughed at her own joke.*
    c   *Soaring nearly 9000 metres into the sky, Everest is the world's highest mountain.*
4   a   *Completed last year, the centre has been a success.*
    b   *Cooked in butter, these mushrooms are delicious.*
    c   *Encrusted with rubies, this is a beautiful necklace.*
5   *The centre, completed last year, has been a success. These mushrooms, cooked in butter, are delicious.*

15 Reports

1   a   the pump room
    b   at the end of the year
    c   the early 1980s
2   a   *Considering its age*
    b   *Refurbished last in the early 1980s*
3   a   The pool linings have been replaced.
    b   *just*
    c   The action is expressed in the present perfect tense.
    d   *will*
4   *the pump room will be refitted, these areas must be given attention*
5   *re*
6   must

16 Settings

1   a   *slowly*
    b   *nervously*
    c   *angrily*
2   a   *a single wooden chair*
    b   Just one chair is available.
    c   Maybe only one chair has been put out to make the narrator feel lonely and isolated.
    d   *cold, hard*
3   a   The adverb suggests the narrator is in no hurry to keep the appointment with the Head. Maybe the narrator is worried.
    b   The adjectives suggest the narrator is feeling very uncomfortable.
4   a   *shuffled*
    b   *glaring, harsh*
    c   The mask seems to be mocking the narrator.

17 Perspective

1   a   Cigarettes are compared with dummies.
    b   The metaphor suggests that smokers are babies – or literally, *suckers*.
2   a   Reality TV is compared to junk food.
    b   The writer considers that both reality TV and junk food are rubbish.
3   a   *Can't be bothered to cook tonight?*
    b   She assumes the answer will be *No*.
4   The adjective should be similar to these: *lazy, idle, pathetic, sad*
5   The writer believes that reality TV is rubbish and the people who watch it are too lazy and idle to do anything else.
6   a   *of course*
    b   *complete*
7   a   *reality*
    b   She is suggesting that reality TV does not reflect reality at all.

18 Speech in literature

1   a   *creepy*
    b   *little girl*
2   a   *he replied*
    b   You would find this structure in books for very young children, perhaps fairy stories.
    c   *said he*
3   *shake*
4   It suggests the woman is trapped (behind bars) and wants to escape.
5   The narrator gets out of bed to feel the wallpaper.
6   She tries to avoid waking John up.
7   She eats properly only when John is there.
8   She was about to say something like *but not better in mind*.

9   **a**   He is talking about his wife as if she is not there.

     b   It is normal if people are not there. It is also normal if the person being talked about is a baby.

19 Phrases and clauses

1   **a**   phrase
     b   clause
     c   phrase
     d   clause
     e   phrase
     f   clause

2   **a**   *she*
     b   *accidents*
     c   *the angry elephant*

3   *some people at the stall*

4   **a**   *The old lady was a happy person who made friends easily.*
     b   *It is a big problem which/that causes lots of disagreements.*
     c   *Think about these people whose lives have been changed.*

5   *The alien was a thoughtful being who always helped others. The alien, who was a thoughtful being, always helped others.*

20 Promotional writing

1   **a**   at the head of the Thames estuary
     b   during the middle of the Victorian era
     c   the buildings

2   **a**   *sits*
     b   *proudly*

3   **a**   Shoebury is described as being at the *head* of the estuary.
     b   This metaphor was probably chosen to suggest a position at the very top of things.

4   **a**   *She*
     b   It makes Shoebury seem more like a living, breathing person.
     c   Ships are sometimes referred to by the same pronoun.

5   **a**   *a crucial role*
     b   *a mighty garrison*
     c   *their superb buildings*

6   **a**   *She has welcomed visitors to these islands for centuries.*
     b   *The town has had a crucial role in our defence against invaders in more recent times. A mighty garrison was settled during the middle of the Victorian era.*

7   **a**   *for centuries*
     b   *during the middle of the Victorian era*

21 Features of narrative

1   **a**   *began*
     b   *smoothly*
     c   *very*

2   **a**   The verb *went* suggests that the whole evening was smooth. The verb *began* indicates that things only started smoothly. They became worse later on.
     b   Nick wanted to prepare the reader for the drama to come.

3   **a**   *The most popular attraction in the entire hall*
     b   *the line of display boards*

4   *dominoes*

5   The younger brothers and sisters

6   *many younger brothers and sisters* to *some of these younger siblings* to *one of them*

7   **a**   The writer says that the work has been destroyed. Of course, it is the display that has been destroyed, not the work of seven years.
     b   Nick uses an exclamation mark to signal his joke.

22 Character in fiction

1   **a**   *slipped quietly*
     b   These actions could suggest many different things about the person: the person could be a thief, a prisoner, or a child in trouble, for example.

2   **a**   *tenderly*
     b   Jonah is cooling his brother's forehead with a wet flannel.
     c   He slips through the door so as not to wake his brother.

3   In the answer to 2c there was much more information to go on. Therefore a much more informed assessment of Jonah's character was possible.

4   *trembling*

5   **a**   *balloon face*
     b   *narrowed eyes*
     c   *uneven yellow teeth*

6   His mouth, his nose and his tongue are also described.

7   The narrator is covered in flecks of spit.

8   There are many possible answers. The answer should be similar to this: *Humbert was an aggressive and unpleasant man.*

23 Instructions and advice

1 *Heat the water until it reaches boiling point.*
2 a *If you boil the water*
   b *Boil the water.*
3 a The adverb suggests that the advice is not absolutely and completely correct.
   b The adverb promises that the absolutely correct advice is just about to be given.
   c Most people can't follow the correct procedure because they cannot measure water temperature with enough accuracy.
4 commas
5 *in fact, in actual fact* (It could even be replaced by *in actuality* but this might sound dated to some people.)
6 If the condition is fulfilled, the tyres will last for years.
7 If the conditions are fulfilled then the temperature of the water will be fine.
8 The writer introduces a personal touch. He talks about his own experiences.

24 Spelling errors

1 a *quiet*
   b *quiet*
   c *quietly*
   d *quite*
   e *quite*
2 *practises, almost, although, quiet, advice, already, quite, all ready, almost, although*

25 Metaphor in Shakespeare

1 a Jaques compares the world to a stage.
   b He extends the metaphor by describing men and women as actors on this stage.
   c The natural time divisions in people's lives are compared to acts in a play.
2 The first age is dominated by crying and being sick.
3 a *creeping*
   b His movement is compared to that of a snail.
4 The schoolboy's face could be shining because he has just had it scrubbed. (Other answers are possible here.)
5 The lover's sighs are compared to a furnace.
6 He sings praises to his lover's eyebrow.
7 A beard is compared to the hair of a leopard. This is a noble and attractive animal.
8 Shakespeare suggests that soldiers are concerned about reputation even in the face of death.
9 *bubble*

26 Test 2

1 a *being, making, going, sleeping, surprising*
   b *been, made, gone, slept, surprised*
2 The final *e* is deleted when *ing* is added.
3 a *Troubled in mind, I cried out.*
   b *Laughing to himself, he walked away.*
   c *Feeling content, we ate our food.*
   d *Covered in dust, the room was silent.*
4 a It is called a rhetorical question.
   b a statistic
   c a quotation
   d *must*
   e imperative
   f a persuasive or argumentative text
5 a The subject of the sentence (cows) has disappeared from the second sentence.
   b It is not needed because, in this case, it doesn't matter who is producing the milk. What is important is that it is being produced.
   c passive
6 a *Corn is grown in the summer.*
   b *Gold is mined in South Africa.*
   c *We were* (or *We have been*) *advised to stop.*
7 a *angrily, bitterly*
   b *barked*
   c an angry dog
   d an adverbial phrase
   e The two prepositions are *of* and *on.*
   f Noun phrases like this are useful because they express a lot of information in an economical way.
8 a *It is a major issue which creates a lot of problems.*
   b *He is a happy animal who loves playing with children.*
   c *This is the injured student whose bravery was so impressive.*
   d *It is a fantastic place which reminds me of great times.*
   e *Come and look at the tree whose roots are causing problems.*

Revision notes